BOOKS BY THE AUTHOR

Forever Free

This title is available as a free eBook at
WiseWordWind.com

Falling Into All

Prayer Sayer Song

Rise Eyes Wise

Prayer Sayer Song

BEN R. TEETER

WISE
WORD
WIND
PRESS

Wise Word Wind Press
P.O Box 371732
San Diego, CA 92137
WiseWordWind.com

Copyright © 2021 by Ben R. Teeter

All rights reserved. Neither this book nor any parts within it may be sold or reproduced in any form without permission.

This is not a work of fiction. Names, characters, places, locations and incidents are all real and are meant to bear a relationship to real-life individuals, living and dead, and actual places, business establishments, locations, events and incidents. Any resemblance to the reader and to those he or she may know is entirely intentional.

Cover Art is a painting by Peter Everly, Untitled, Copyright 1988, used by permission.

Cover Design by Randy Gibbs

Book Layout by Golden Ratio Book Design

First Edition

Printed in the United States of America

ISBN: 978-1-7349891-8-2 (Trade Paperback)
ISBN: 978-1-7349891-5-1 (Ebook)
ISBN: 978-1-7349891-6-8 (Hardcover)

Library of Congress Control Number: 2021913412

ACKNOWLEDGMENT

O

Like
A
Flock
Of
Birds,

A
Block
Of
Words

Has
Landed

Chirping,
Singing,

In
This
Place,

This
Heart
Space,

Here,

Where
All
Things
Be.

And

I
Am
Kissed

Once
Again

By
Thee.

PREFACE

O
Thou,

Prayer
Sayer,

Now
Prayer
Say.

Let
Peace

Descend

Upon
The
Day.

Prayer Sayer Song

A
Sanctuary

Now
Befalls,

One
Without
Walls,

Or
Priestly
Calls,

A
Silent
Bliss,

This,

A
Melody

Of
Awes.

I
Ask
No
Boon.

I
Ask
No
Healing.

I
Ask
No

Special
Thought

Or
Feeling.

I
Ask
For

Only
You,

O
Perfect
True.

You
Drop
In

And
There
Is
A
Burning

Hole
In
My
Day,

Taking

All

Time
Away.

O
Ignited
Moment,

Stay.

One
Breath

From
You,

And

The
Veils
Between
Us

Flutter

And
Are
Gone.

Peace

Pours
In

Upon

My
Crumbling
Questions.

O
Infinite
One,

Might
I
Have
A
Moment
Of
Your
Time,
Please?

O
Thank
You!

This,
Your
Time.

The
Moment.

Satisfies

What
I
Had
Thought

Were
Needs.

I
Would
Read

The
Falling
Of
The
Dew,

Each
Clear
Sphere

Condensing

In

The
Evening
Cool,

Another
Word

From
You.

I
Steal
A
Moment

From
The
Day,

To
Hear
What
You

May
Have
To
Say.

And
You
Strum

The
String
Of
Everything.

I
Listen
To

You
Play.

Still

will
I
Sit.

And
Be.

And
Dwell

In
Thee.

Becoming

The
Empty
Place

In
Your
Flute

I
Hear
The
Singing
Sound

Abound.

I
Sink
Into

Your
Silent
Breath,

The
Sense
Of

Sacred
Rest

Profound.

Choruses

Of

Angels'
Calls

Fill
The
Halls

Within

My
Ears.

O
Throng,

Sing
Psalm
Song

O

So
Strong.

Please,

Flood
My
Rivers.

Break
My
Banks.

Deepen
Me.

Let
This
Secret
Love,

Disguised
As
Ordinary
Things,

Out.

Let
This

Gentle
Happiness

Tenderly

Shout.

River
Follows

Valley
Walls.

Ocean

Calls.

O
Clarity,

My
Sweet
Friend,

May
You

Never
End.

I
Sit.

Open.

Release

Soul's
Skin.

Let
All

In.

O

Unto
The
Perfect,

Surrender,

O
Lovely

Ascender.

Entering
Into

The
Absolute
Home,

The
Heavens
Mere

Appear

As
The
Yard
Outside,

While
Here

Inside

The
Om

Rest
I,

The
Infinite
Tall,

Infinite
Wide.

Peace
Falls

Upon
A
Soul

Like
Evening
Air

In
Tall
Pines

Upon
The
Mountain.

What
Prayer
Is
This?

Where
God
Descends

Upon
The
Man,

Washing
Away

All
Word,

And
Only

The
Rushing
Of
Washing

Is
Heard.

And,

Once
Again

I
Stand,

Firmly
Caught

By
You,

After
Treading
Beyond

Another
Precipice,

Where
Was

Nought.

In
Pre-
Dawn
Dim

I
Sing
My
Hymn

To
You,

O
Ever
Perfect
True,

To
Ensure

That
This,

My
Own

Rising
Morn,

Is
Born,
Too,

As

The
Perfect

All
Through.

Nothing
More

Than
This

Do
I
Need

To
Do.

O
Listen.

A
Sea

Without
A
Shore

Does
Not
Strike

Or
Roar.

O,

Here
Lift

Another

Wisp
Adrift

In
Thy

Infinity.

The
Dove

Of
Your
Love

Descends,

The
Size
Of
Sky.

And,
O,

You

Become

I.

Love

May
Rush

Into
Words.

Or
May

Linger

In
Glances.

While
Ever,

Love

In
All
Things

Dances.

Now
Advancing,

Love
Comes
Marching
In,

Taking
All,

Holding
All
Prisoner

In
This
Cage,

A
Brilliant
Dancing
Cage,

This,

Of
Bliss.

Glorious
Thou
Art.

Beyond
All
Glories,
Too.

O,
Silent,

Perfect
True,

O,

The
Man

Goes
Falling,

Falling
Into
You.

Grace
And
Gratitude

Merge
As
One

Father
Bequeaths
All

With
No
Exceptions

To
The
Son.

Allow
Me
Please

To
Touch,

Be
Touched
By,

Another
Aspect
Of
You

Today,

And

Sit
Ringing,

A
Hole

In
Your
Flute,

So
Empty.
So
Full.

O,
Low
I
Bow

Before
Thee,
Lord.

I
But
Adore.

I
Sink
Into
Thy
Floor.

Here
Alone

Before
Thy
Throne.

O,
Sun,

Whence
Ever

All

Hath
Shone.

Let
Me
Be

Attached

But
To

Only
You,

O,

Ever
Perfect
True.

Let
Here
Pour

For
Us

A
Lore

More
Pure

Than
Heretofore.

Let
Us

See
The
Grace

Before
Our
Face,

Now

As
The
Real.

The
Perfect.
Sure.

A
Breeze
Of
Ease.

May

A
Strain
Of
Pain.

Bring
Truth
Plain.

Either
Of
These

Then
Let
This

Mortal
Puppet
Man,

Doing
His
Normal
Daily
Things,

Dance
On
These
Immortal
Perfect
Strings.

And
So
Now

All
Of
Life,

So
Easy,

Sings.

O

This
Morning
Moment

Is

My
Mountain,
High.

I
Call.

A
Vision
Quest

Is
Nigh.

And,
O,

Now,

Visions
Tumble

From
The
Sky.

Your
Dove

Of
Peace

Arrives,

Pecks,

Picks,

The
Seeds,

and
Worms,

From
This,

The
Flower
Bower

In
My
Heart.

This
Adam
Atom

Spins
On
Man
Me,

Casting
Forth,

Awhirl,

A
World,

A
Universe,

In
This

The
Brilliance

Of
Mine
Own

Infinity.

For
The
Butterfly

The
World

Is
A

Bright
Color

Nectar
Scented

Place

In
A

Warm
And
Hovering

Sky.

Let
The
Peace

Of

Eternal
Patience

Invade

The
Soul

And

Make
This

The
Moment

Whole.

In
Sacred
Rest   Hear

Profound,   All
                        Sound.

I
Become

The
Empty
Place

In
Your
Silence

And

I
Am

So
Blessed.

Even
Now,

Your
Song
Birds

Startle,

Singing
Forth

Within
My
Breast.

And

You
Take
Me
To

A
Perfect
Rest.

Seeing

Being
The
Infinity

Takes
The
Breath
Away,

Takes
The
Death

Away.

Hear

Angel
Sing,

Atom
Ring,

Humming
Of
Sun's
Bell,

Radiating,

Fabricating,

Every
Thing,

Perfection

Now
To
Tell.

You
Bless.

Gone
Is
My
Stress.

And

Soft
The
Sound

Of

Angel
Wings

Is
Messaging

The
Grace

Within
All
Things.

O
Feel
Joy
Abound,

Springing
From

The
Very
Ground

That
Sings.

Saints
And
Sages,

Here
Arrayed,

Outside

Of

Time's
Parade,

You
Are

Flower
Stars

The
One

Has
Made,

Each
Of
You

A
Kiss

Of
Bliss.

You
Glow,

Heart
Not
Apart.

You
Show

Life

In,
As,

The
Perfect
One

Is
This.

The
Man

Feels
You,

O
Perfect
One,

O
God,

Pervade
and
Dissolve

The
Clod,

The
Earth,

That
He
Had
Made
Of
Self.

So
Odd.

Now
Are

Earth's
Atoms

Gone
As

Glimmering
Stars

In
Night
Sky.

And

Now,
One
Sky.

One
Glimmer.

One
Atom
Star,

All
Things

Are.

Brilliance
Perfect,

Light
Of
All,

Man
Doth
Fall
To
Knee

Before
Thee

Lost

In
Awe.

My
House

Is
Burning
Down.

No
Place

To
Lay
My
Head.

So,

I
Will
Rest

Upon
This
Pillow

Of
The
Stars

Instead.

And,

You
Showed
Me
That

Spirit
Is
The
Durable,

And
These

So
Solid
Seeming

Elements
Of
Earth

Are
The
Soft
And
Fleeting

Shadows
In
A
Dream.

O
See
Them

Stream,

Bubbles
In
A
Brook,

Gone

Before
You
Can
Even

Take
A
Look.

Mind
Is
In
Thee
A-
Roam.

Now,
Like
A
Rising,
Balloon,
It
Finds,

At
Atmosphere
Top,

Its
Skin
Disappears

With
A
Pop!

And

All
Of
The
Universe,

Home.

O
Man,

But

Rest,

And

Abide
In
The
True.

The
Infinite
One

Is
Being
You.

Here
Is
One

Pin-
Point
Dot.

One

Sphere
Center
Spot,

With
Versions
Everywhere,

Identical.

So
Radiates

Everywhere

The
One
Self.

And
So,

Around
This
Me
Now,

Is

A
Myriad
World

Begot.

There
Is
Such
Surplus

In
All
Things

That
I
Asked
For.

So
Much
More

Than
I
Might
Store,

And

Surprises
Still
Arrive,

Heaped,

At
The
Door.

We
Sing
And
Dance

Upon
The
Rainbow
Stair

That
You
Have
Cast

Upon
The
Air,

The
Steps

Whereon

We
Rise,

To
Be
With
Thee,

Wise,

Aware.

The
Man
Is
Stunned.

"One-ed."

Oneness

Suddenly
Occurs.

Grace
Is
Felt

Within
The
Daily

Race
For
Bread.

Limits

Fall
Away.

The
All-
Time
Appears,

And,

Where
Were
Subtle
Fears,

Deep
Love
Instead.

Infinitude,
Here,

You
Appear,

Touch

My
Mind.

You
Are

So
Perfect.

Kind.

My
Head
Is

An
Empty
Bowl.

A
Cup.

A
Satellite
Dish

Turned
Up

To

Only
You.

I
Saw
Thy

Message

Where
You
Wrote
It

On
The
Sky,

White
On
Blue,

So
Delicate
A
Feathering,

A
Soft
Subtle
Wing
Of
Calligraphy

Adrift

Upon
The
High.

I
Stumble

From

Guidance
To
Guidance,

Ever
Feeling

Somewhat

Unaware,

Yet
Ever

Feeling

You,

O
Perfect
One,

Are
There.

I
See
You

Dancing

In
The
Trees'

Infinities.

I
Feel
You

Touch

So
Sweetly

in
The
Breeze.

I
Feel
You

Magnify

This
Soul

And
Make

It

As

The
Whole,

In
The

Utter
Ease.

After
Rain,

Roses
Bloom.

After
Pain,

Love
Has

More
Room.

Please,

Burst
Upon
Us,

O,
Wondrous
All.

Or,

Slowly
Dawn,

Awaken
Us
Softly,

Until

All
The
Night

Is
Gone.

Let
The
Man

Come
To

Succumb
To

You,

O
Perfect
True.

Whenever
Any

Quandary,
Quagmire,

Lack
Of
Clue,

We
Surrender
Unto

You,
O
Perfect
True,

For
Each

Quest
Or
Question
Or
Request,

We
Find

The
Answer

Doth
Ensue.

Man
Cannot
Sit

With
You,

O
Sweet
One,

In
This

Flood
Of
Bliss.

Troubles
Of
The
Day

Wash
Quite
Away,

And,

Gone
Too,

The
Man,

We
Shall
Not
Miss.

There
Is
Something

Breathed

That
Is
Not
Air.

A
Breath

Beyond
This

Life
And
Death

Is
There.

Its
White
Wings

Rise
And
Fall,

Carry

Soul

Softly

Into
All.

Hear?

There!

Delicate
And
Fair

An
Angel's
Trumpet
Blare

Is
Soft

Upon
The
Air.

And
You

My
Questions
Answer,

One
By
One,

The

Cosmic
And
Mundane.

In
Answering,

The
Question
Gone,

And,

Only
You

Remain.

If
I
May

Set
 Down
This
Load

And
Sit
Awhile
With
You

And

Feel
You
Near,

Then
All
The
Day

Will
Pass

Sweet,

As
I
See

All
Things
Your
Body
Are.

Sky,
Events,
Attitudes.

The
Sand
Grains
In
The
Street.

I
Sometimes

Do
Not
Hold

My
Harmful
Tongue

When
I
Am

Out
Among

The
Other
Drivers

Of
The
Cars.

I
Become

A
Denizen
Of
Mars.

A
Fire-
Breather

Roaring

To
Protect

A
Metal
Skin.

I
Fail
Sometimes

To
Pause

And

Let
Love
In.

I
Would
Put
Away

The
Books
Of
Man,

And
Read
Instead
The
Lines

Upon

The
Wind.

And
Sit
And
Listen
To
The
Call,

The
Singing,

Of
The
All.

The
Hurrying
Moment

Dissolves

Into

The
Still

One.

Split
Of
Self

Healed.

Self,
World,
God,

One.

And
A
War

That
Never
Was

Need
Not

Be
Won.

The
Eternalness

Within
This
Body

Looks
Out

From
These
Eyes,

Now

Existing
In

What
They
See,

All

Quietly
Rearranging

As
Everything.

Infinitely.

Let
All
That
Vibrates

Cease,
Be
Still.

Let
Mote
In
Eye

Be
Cast
Away.

Let
I
Behold

In
Awe

The
Allness,
All,

No
Wall,

No
Flaw.

O
Now
Behold,

No
Sigh
Today.

O
Man

Go
Anywhere,

And
You
Shall
Find,

Already
There,

The

Aware.

A
World
Of

Half-
Truth,

Error,

Conflict-
Cursed,

Is
An
Urging
Home

To
The
True,

In
Which

It
Is

Immersed.

Dear
One,

You
Come
Flowing

Like
A
Brook

Over
My
Stones,

And
Make
Them

Shine
And
Sing.

You
Come
Blowing

Like
A
Wind

Through
These
Bones,

And
Make
Me

Everything.

In
Seeing

Each
Wisp

Of
Each
Feather

Of
Each
Sparrow

So
O
Perfect!

The
Beloved
One

Now
Flies,

Arrives,
In
The
Sight

Of
These
Eyes.

Dear
God,

It
Is
So
Odd

How
Blind
My
Mind

Can
Be.

The
Infiniteness

All
Around

In
Everything

How
Do
I

Often

Fail
To
See?

Mountain
Mover,

You
Mold
Mountains,

Moment
To
Moment.

To
You,

They
Are

Soft
As
Sunsets,

Fleeting
As
Ideas.

All
That
Solid
Rock

In
Rolling
Waves

Like
A
Sea.

So,
O
Mountain

Boulder
Molder,

Please

Mold
Me.

I
Lose
The
Urge

For
More,

For,

It
Is
Clear,

Already,

All

Is
Here.

I
Alter
Myself.

I

Altar

My
Self.

I
Lift
Up

An
Empty
Cup

To
You,

And
You

Fill
It

Up

Again.

Anew.

Feeling
You
There,

I
Do
Not
Think

Of
This

Friendship,

O
Perfect
One,

As
Prayer.

Breath's
Undulating
Flutter,

Nerve's
Sparkling
Sputter,

Mind's
Endless
Mutter,

I
Surrender
These

To
You.

Do
With
Them

As
You
Please,

O,
Perfect
True.

Sky
Comes
Landing

In
This
Nest

Built
Of
Sticks,

Length
Limitless,

Bird
Gone.

When
Going
Up

Before

The
Perfect
Judge,

Do
Not
Fudge.

Speak
Clear.
Sincere.

Don't
Budge.

And
He

Will
Respect
You

And
Revere.

And
I
Feel
You

Gather
Me

Into
You,

And
You
Cast

My
Old
Sorrows

Into

Perfect
Todays

And

Loving
Tomorrows.

Everything-
Ness

Permeates.

O
Let
Your
Perfection

Be
My
Star,

Leading
Me

To

Where
You
Are.

And
You

Take
These
Stones

Of
My
Old

Dungeon
Walls,

That
I

Have
Built
So

Carefully
Around
Me,

To
Surround
Me,

And   A
Each   Bright
Bursts   Place

Like   Where
A   You
Star,   Are.

Becoming

And
Now

The
Person

Who
Thinks
That
He
Matters

Shatters.

And
All
The

Gathering
Of
Generic
Parts,

All
Of

His
Old
Being,

Scatters.

Yet
Again,

Another
Cycle
Turns.

Day
Begins.

Sun
Burns.

Nature's
Creature
Yearns.

Mortal
Man
Learns.

And
Yet
Again,

A
Prodigal

Returns.

The
Darkest
Dark,

The
Coldest
Cold,

Occur

Before
The
Dawn
Is
Born.

Hope

Rises
Out

From
Hopelessness,

The
Deepest
Fall
Forlorn.

Man
Reaches
Out

When

He
Is
Down.

He
Begs

When
He
Has
None.

He
Lives
At
Last,

When

The
Arrogance
Is
Done.

I
See
Here

Your
Crop
Of
Man

Upon
This
Mortal
Plain.

Here,
Pleasure,
Pain

Are
Sun
And
Rain

That
Bring
Forth

Waving
Field,

Rich
And
Golden
Yield,

Each   In
Brightening   Your
Head   Breeze.

Grown
Fragrant,
Full,

And
Sure
To
Please,

Now
Moving
All
Together

We,

Your
Sweet
Baby,

Cuddle
Here

In
Your
Arms,

Peacefully
Asleep,

Or
Crying

And

Fitfully
Fussing

Our

Urgent
And
Hungry

Alarms.

Mind
In
Prayer,

Resting
There.

Every
Duty
Done.

No
More

Travail
On
Trail.

A
Speck

Has
Flown

Unto

The
Center

Of

The
Sun.

O.

Love
Has
Become
Fact.

Inseparable

From

Any
One
Act.

Breath
Rolls
In

Breath
Rolls
Out

Herein
I
Feel

Only
You

Bringing
This
About.

Let
Me
Not

Mindless
Mutter,

Utter,
Prayer

To
The
Air.

Let
Me
Not

Cry
High,

Sigh
For
Thee,

As
If

More
Far

Than
Any
Star

You
Are.

But

Let
Me
Quiet

Sit
And
Be

O
Nearest
Dear,

With
You,

And

This,

The
Simply
True.

Under
The
Guise

Of
Normal
Life,

A
Common
Man

With
Job
And
Wife

Strips
His
Soul

To
Barest
Skin

To
Let
You
In,

Relinquishing
All
Strife,

Surrendering
Again.

Again.

Again.

Your
Consolations

Arrive

Unexpected,

Like
A

Package
At
The
Door,

Or

A
Sudden
Call,

From

All.

Hello!
It
Is

Free
Tech
Support

From
Heaven,

Twenty-
Four-
Seven.

And
So,

I
Fall

More
Deeply

Into

Gratitude
And
Awe.

Imagine,

O
Man,

If
You
Dare,

That

The
All,

Before
You
There,

Is
All
Aware.

And

Looks
Upon
You

Now.

With
Care.

I
Close
My
Eyes

And
Fall

Into

Your
Pure

Night
Skies.

I
Cast
My
Word

Like
Rising
Dust

That
Lets

The
Wind

Be
Seen.

It
Falls
Again.

And

All
Is

Pristine.

Truth,
Kind,

Washes
The
Mind

That
Was
Blind.

Nectar
Is

Where
Was

Only
Rind.

Rising,

Falling,

This

Breath
Of
Me

Becomes
A
Wave

Of
The

Eternal
Sea.

I
Install
This

Altar

In
My
Soul.

And
Here

I
Fall

Before
You.

All

Grows
Clear

And

Whole.

Elijah
Sat

With
Only
You,

Upon
A
Barren
Hill,

Among

Dry
Sticks
And
Sand

And

You
Gave
Him,

In
A
Raven's
Bill,

A
Morsel

For
His
Meal.

He
Saw
It

Arrive
There

In
Your
Hand.

Real.

I
Shall
Not
Pursue

This
Vain
Avenue,

A
Form
Of
Living,

Leading
Not

To
You.

O
Man,

Each
Decision

Is
A
Stroke

In
The
Swim

Toward

'Him.'

Where
Next?

I
Ask.

Only
Here,

You
Answer.

Riding
The
Wave

Of
The

Opening
Bloom,

I
Feel

Limitings

Rise.

I
Feel

Openings

Of
Eyes,

Unlimited
Room.

The

Hold
Of
Form

So
Very
Strong
Is,

Until
At
Last,

It
Softens,

And,
Form,
Place,

Is
Held

Within
The
Hand

Of

Purest
Empty
Space.

And
Then,

They

Hold
Each
Other.

Perfect

Embrace.

In

The
One

God
Is
The
See

In
Which
I
See.

God
Is
The
Be

In
Which

I
Be.

God
Is
The
Me

In
Which

I
Me.

One
Is.

Two
Reflects.

Zero
Perfects.

You
Have
Guided

The
Rich
Man

On
His
Camel

To
The

Eye
Of
Needle.

He
Has
Dismounted

And

Given
All
Away.

The
Mustard
Seed

Goes
Flying
Through

Today.

I
Dance
Out

To
Seeing
You.

I
Dance
In

To
Being
You.

Feeling
Us
Play

This,

Being's
Flute,

Now
Are
All
Questions

Moot.

The
Dark
Veil
Lifts,

Transforms

Into
Sail,

Or
Wing,

That
Can
Bring

All
Home,

Who
Were
Aloof.

Alone.

I
Only
Yearned.

But
Then

I
Burned.

I
Burned
Away

The
Scrambled,
Brambled,

Overgrowth
Of

Plan
Of
Man,

And,
In
This,

Earned

An
Emptiness,

Under,
In,

Your
Sweet

Vast
And
Naked

Sky.

And

Here
We
Meet,

You
And
I.

The
Worries

I
Was
Wont

To

Keep
And
Grow,

Are
Now

Springs
And
Rivulets

Where

Your
Blessings
Flow.

And
You
Show
Me:

The
Mars

Of
Cars,

And
Iron
Things,

And
Wars,

And
Hammerings,

Is
Also
He

Who
Drives

The
Soul

Home
To
Thee.

Air
Breaks
Open.

And

The
All
Is
Here.

Size
Is
Not.

And
Now,

Time
Is
Not
Broken

Fore
And
Aft.

And
Man,
Now

No
Cobbled
Raft,

But
Ocean
All,

And
Now
Is
Body
But

A
Wick

Beneath

Perfection's

Flame
Of
Light.

Now
Is

No
Day.

No
Night.

The

Walls
Of
Time

Are
Hard
As
Stones.

Man
Cannot
Move
The
Day

Wherein

He
Is
Obliged
To
Stay.

But
Soul
May

Melt
Away

All

Wall
Stone,

And
See

No
Flesh,
No
Bone,

And,

With
Angelic
Wing

And

Singing
Tone,

Be
In
Thee,

O,
Ever
True,

Free,
In
The

Infinity.

Limits
Burn
Away.

Quiet
Soul.

Endless
Space.

A
Wisp
Of
Bindings,

Once
A
Man,

Trail
Off
In

A

Breeze
Of
Grace.

This,

The
Forever,

Is

Long
Enough

For

What
Is

To
Work
Out.

O
God,

I
Dare.

I
Raise
My
Eyes.

I
Praise.

And
You

Raise
Me
There,

Unto
You,

And,

All
Of
You,

You
Share.

Great
Sky
Eye

I

Opens

Ocean
Wide.

With

No
Tide.

Dear
One,

I
Have
Gone

Into

The
Wayside
Bramble.

I
Feel
The
Bite

Of

Many
A
Small
Snare,

Holding
Me
There.

Please

Arrive
And
Release

Your
Dear
One,

Back

Into
The
Track,

Into
The
Peace

Of

Your
Care.

And
You
Show
Me

The
Feeling
Of

The
Razor's
Edge,

For,

This
Narrow
Path

Permits
No

Slip
And
Fall,

Without

A
Deep
Cutting

Of

The
All

Back
Into
Two,

Taking
Me

Away

From
You.

Gratitude...

Grace...

Bliss...,

...Rise.

...Fall.

...Kiss.

Let
Me

Sing
As
Thee,

O

Perfect

Forever
Free.

O
God,

Perfect
Complete
Infinite
One,

The
Man
Has
Meandered,

And
Now,

Caught,

Calls
To
You,

From
The
Thicket

Of
His
Own

Thought.

Goddess
Stands,

Peaceful
Face,

Arm
Slung
Over

Pouring
Vase.

All
That
Pours,

Is
Empty
Space.

Statue
Stone,

Carved
Grace.

The
Garment,

O
God,

You
Give
To
Me,

This
Gorgeous
Gift,

Infinity,

Now
I
See,

Is
But

The
Gift
Wrap.

For,

You
Give
Now

Quiescent

The

Very
Heart

Of
Thee.

O
God,

You
Bring

Man
On
Knees

To
Ease,

Releasing
Pain.

No
Word

Occurred,

That
Could

Explain.

The
Perfect
True

Is
Perfect
Kind.

So,
O
Man,

But
Ask.

Release
Task.

Bask.

Unwind.

No

Thing
Here.

Only

The
Infinite.

The
Perfect.

Dear.

And
You,

O
Perfect
One,

Moved
All
Things,

Aside

Out
Of
My
Way,

So
I
Could
Be

With
Only
You

Today.

Long
Did
I

Project
The
Lord

As
Far
Away
On
High.

Until,
One
Day,

I
Spoke,
Dear.

And
So,
I

Awoke.

With
You,
God,

Near.

And,
Then
Inside,

Precisely
Where

I
Used
To
Hide.

And
Then
You
Purified

My
Eye,

So

I
Could
See

You
Are

The
All
Of
Me,

And
The
Infinity

In
Which
I
Ride.

Let
Every
Prayer
Sayer

Raise
Now
Word
Wise.

Let
Earth
Now
Mend.

Let
Man
Now
Rise,

Amend,
Ascend,

Feel
And
Be,

Widest
Skies.

Simple
Word
Heard.

Eye
Edgeless
Sky.

Heart
Soaring
Bird.

Even

A
Black
Wick,

A
Mere
Dried
Up
Stick,

May

Calmly
Humbly
Stand,

Not
Grand,

And

Hold
The
Flame,

For

The
Warmth
And
Light

That
Takes
Away

The
Night.

Pairs
Of
Bones

Upon
A
Space,

A
Body

Temple
Place.

In
Stately
Pace

Blossom
Opens
Now
In
Grace.

Let
The
Clear

Here
Inhere

In
Human
Race.

Sweet
One,

You
Have
Revealed

That

Only
You

Are
Being
Me.

The
Infinity

Is
Intimate.

And
This
Breath,

The

Eternity.

I
Did
Not
Know

My
Feet

Were
Climbing
So,

But
Now
I
See

A
Mountain

You
Have
Raised

Here
Under
Me.

And

I
Am
Free.

You

Lift
A
Mountain

Beneath
Me.

The
Still
Air

Sings.

Sacredness
Shows

Shining

In
All
Things.

I
Throw
Out

All
My

Figuring
Out.

I
Decide

To
Have
You,

All-
Being,

Guide.

Your
Limo

Is
The
Softest
Ride.

Like
Arjuna,

I
Find

My
Driver,
The
Divine.

And
So,

All
Battle
Yet
To
Come,

Already
Won.

Grim
Jaws
Of
Death,

A
Doorway
Filled
With
Angel
Breath.

Every
Loss

That
Thunders

But

A

Lightening
Of
Load,

For
One

Already
In

The
Infinite

Palatial

Abode.

Peace
Pours
In.

Gone
Now
Humble,

I
Find

All
My
Questions

Crumble.

Only
The
Infinite

Is,

Everywhere
I
Look.

How
Can
I
Not

Be
That?

The
Bones
Balance

Upon
Emptiness.

Man
Becomes
Nave.

Gone

Is
Slave.

One
Touch

From
You,

O
Perfect
True,

My
Chains

Are
Changed.

My
Trouble
Mind
Is
Gone.

My
Body

Fills
With
Light.

My
Genes
Are
Rearranged.

The   Spans
Slaver's   The
Binds   Night.

Are
Now
Festoons,

Royal
Decorations
Bright.

Our
Wingspan

We,
Man,

We
Wander,

And
You
Cast
Before
Us

Your
Manna,

Your
Quail,

And

You
Cast
Before
Us

The
Pearls

That

Turn
Swine
Into
Men.

O
You
Guide

And

Your
Treasure

You
Give

Without
Measure.

Again.

Again.

Even
Now,

Each
Of
These
Humans

Is
Rounding

Their
Own
Way

Toward
Their

Perfect
Doorway

Moment
In
Time,

That
Is

The
Surest

Part
Of
Them.

Even

Your
Form

As

The
Without
Number

Cannot

Contain
You.

My
Concepts
Melt,

And
My
Goals.

This
Chair

Becomes
Your
Palm.

The
Atoms

Gathered
Here
As
Me,

Pose
Perfect

On
Their
Centers,

You.

Stillness
And
Motion

Merge.

The
Unfinished

Loses

All
Urge.

This
Shape
Of

Soul
Skin

That
Seems
To
Hold

All
The
Me

Within,

Now
Seems
To
Be
Very
Thin.

How
Can
I
Tell?

Where
Does
It
End?
Begin?

Sweet
One,

You
Glide
In

Upon
The
Singing

Of
My
Breath

And

Steal
Me

Away

With
You.

I
Feel
You

Embrace
Me

In
Each
Form

I
Occupy,
Or
Wear,

Warming
Me

Into
Existence

So

Softly,

Sometimes
I
Forget

Your
Touch

Is
There.

I
Hold
Up

This
Dry
Old
Wick.

Let
Love
Light
Here.

Let
This

Dark
And
Heavy

Matter
Mere

Burn

Bright.

Clear.

I
Feel

A
Breath
Infinite

Enter
Here
Today,

Where

Here-
To-
Fore

Was

Only
Clay.

O
Man,

Remember,

It
Is
All

Watching,
Connected,

Loving,

Waiting
To
See

Only

Your
Searching
Eyes.

Thrown
Out

From
Its
Harness,

This
Horse

Discovers
Pegasus
Wings,

Rides
Out.

Rides
Up.

Sings.

Let
This
Small
Piece

Of

What
Is
There

Dare

Release
Bolder.

Be
Bare.

Be
Peace
Of
Continuum,

The
One

All
Aware.

A
Seed
Husk,
Soft,
Bursts.

A
Compaction
Of
Plant
Complete

Unfurls,
Unfolds,

Tossing
Off

Carapace
Cap,

An
Exuberant
Graduate,

Green-
Gowned.

The
New
Plant
Child

Emerges,

Pure,
Replete,

From
The
Ground.

O
Man

In
Wandering
Dryness,

Desert
Sand,

You
Are

The
Moses,

Rod
In
Hand.

Strike
The
Rock

While
The
Hard-
Hearted
Stand.

Let
Life
Love
Flow.

Water
The
Land.

My
Bones
Melt

In
This

Morning
Light,

Like
Drops
Of
Dew,

Evaporating,

Back
To
You.

Neighbors
Appear,

With
Loving

Smiles
And
Words,

Where
Before
Were

Only
Strangers

And

Startled
Birds.

I
Ever
Err.

There
Is
Nowhere

This
Is
Not
So,

So,
Let
This

Flow
Of
Error

Be
The
Fuel,

Be
The
Tool,

That
Ever
Leads
Me

Back
To
Thee,

In
Constantly
Correct

Humility.

Sky
Has
Cracked
Open,

Wide
And
Ripe.

Fragments
Sweet,

Objects
Ordinary

Turn
Iconic
As

Monument,
Amulet,
Altar,

Temple
Space.

The
Air
Is
Charged

With

Mystery
And
Grace.

Good
And
Evil

Merge
In
Struggle,

Back
As
One

In
Thee.

Another
Human
Soul

Is
Free.

The
Very
Substance

Of

The
Night

Is

Burning
Bright.

Let
Me
Join

The

Lilies
Of
The
Field,

Bowing
In
Your
Breeze,

Moving

Infinitely

Subtly.

As
You
Please.

Mists
Lift.

One
More
Stepping
Stone

Is
Shone.

You
Come

As
Friend,

As
Guide,

As
Teacher,

Healer,

As
Strong
Ally,

To
Stand,

Walk,

At
My
Side.

The
Path

Opens
Wide.

Dawn,
Now,

Cannot
Hide.

One
Breath

From
You

And

All
The
Veils

Between
Us

Flutter,

And
Are
Gone.

Soul's
Skin
Collapses

In
Your
Presence,

And
The
Skin

Within
That
Skin.

Veils
Blow,

And
Then

Blow
Away.

Only
You

Here
Today.

I
Sit
In
This
Quiet

Hallway
Intersection,

Where

Past
And
Future

Stretch
Away

Oppositely,

And
I
Ignite

And
Light
Them

From
This
Bursting
Soul

With
Love

And

They
Are
Joined
Whole,

No
More
Stretched
Out

As
Lonely
Pathways
Ever
Stringing.

And
Now

The
All

With
A
Shout.

Is
Singing.

And
You
Give
Me

This,

Your
Burden.

And
It
Is

So
Light,

It
Lifts!

And
All
Is

But

Your
Gifts.

Joy
Breaks,

Casting
Beauty
Every
Where,

Like
Fine
Dawn,

Strewing
Jewels

On
The
Lawn.

Choose
Carefully

Each
Word
You
Say.

Each
One
May

Modify

The
Deep
Foundation

Of
The
Day.

The
Mind

May
Go

At
Last

Into

Permanent
Prayer.

No
Thought.

No
Word.

No
Image.

No
Sayer.

The
Moment,

Now
New,

Opens,

Like
An
Empty
Page,

Ready
For
A
Touch,

An
Empty
Stage

Awaiting

Actor's
Foot
And
Voice.

The
New.

The
Empty.

The
Now.

Full
Of
Choice.

This
Moment

Is
Such.

No
Need
To

Prove

The
True.

No
Need
To

Improve

The
Perfect.

No
Need
To

Enlarge

The
All.

Gratitude

Bursts
Me,

Like

A
Bright
Rising
Balloon,

A
Bubble,

A
Blossom.

This
Pearl

Is
Cast,

Divine,

Here,

Where
Are

No
Swine.

No
Need

For
Special
Place.

No
Need

For
Special
Time.

No
Need
For
Special
Things,

No
Objects
Of

A
Special
Kind.

This
Moment
Now

Is
Fine.

Only
The
All

Could
Make
This
Man.

Only
The
Perfect

Complete
Plan.

Only

An
Infinite
Array

Could
Make
This
Day.

Only

The
Perfect,

It
Is
Clear,

Is
What
Is

Ever
Here.

Infinity's

Poise
Point

Appears
Now

In,
As,

Me.

Ordering,

Stilling,

The
Cacophony.

The
Man
Is

Filled
In
With

The
Infinite
Small,

And
Surrounded
By

The
Infinite
Tall.

His
Frail

Bubble
Boat

Sensory
Sphere,

Afloat
Here,

Is
Only

Ocean

After
All.

Life
Is
Not

Explainable,
Containable.

Mind
Must
Surrender,

Resolving
By
Dissolving,

Tender,

To

The
True,

And
Join.

Only
A
Fool

Continues

With
The
Wrong
Tool

For
The
Task.

If
You
Want
To
Know

Life,

Just
Approach.

Nicely.

Ask.

Timeless

Infinite
Perfection

No
Where

Rolls
In,

To
Hide.

Flood
Tide.

Personality

Now
Has

Let
Nerves

Fall
Still

As

Winter
Tree

On
Wind-
Less

Starry
Night.

Stillness
Falls

Upon
The
Waves.

Freedom
Spreads

Among
The
Slaves.

Brightness

Bursts

In

All
The
Caves.

Infinity
Dawns

Upon
The
View,

In
Every
Direction

Looked
Into,

Spreading
Open

Mind,

Here-
To-
Fore

Contained,

And

Blind.

Heart's
Tight
Knot

Appears

Loosens.

Between

The
Windings.

Falling
Away

Are
Bindings.

Open
Sky

Let
Me
See
Thee,

O
My
Soul,

As
Thou
Art,

Non-
Existent,

Except

As

The
Total

Whole.

You
Would,

O
Man,

Protect
A
Sacred
Space,

A
Sacred
Way,

A
Way

Particular

To
Pray,

A
House,

A
Word,

A
Hat,

A
Cloak,

A
Certain
Special

Scented
Smoke,

But
Know,

The
Sacred
Is

Already
All,

And
Holds
You

Safe
Today,

Despite
What-
Ever

You
May
Do

And
Say.

A
Man
Meanders

For
A
While,

Then,

Marches
Forward
To

The
Ever
True.

For,
Now,

The
Asides

Will
Never
Do.

Infinity
A-
Dance

Before,
Within,
My
Eyes.

Leaves
Of
Grass
And
Trees

Quake,
Shake,

Swing,
Upon
The
Breeze.

These
Infinities

Bring
My
Mind,

Bring
Me,

To
Knees.

Another
Turn

Of

All
That
Turns.

Another

Day,
Moment,
Thought.

And,

O,

Once
Again,

Perfect
Center

That
Was
Sought,

Caught.

O
Look!

Sky
Has
Landed!

Here
We
Are

Among
This

Lovely

Scattering
Of
Star.

No
More
Is

The
Infinite

Afar.

O
The
Beauty

Of

The
Blossoming

Of
Man,

When
Soul

Blows
Open

Unto
Starry
Sky

And

God-
Filled
Eye.

No
Mere
Body

Can

Disguise

Heart
Gone

Over-
Flowing

Wise,

After
So
Many

Starts
And
Tries.

The
Cosmic
Water

Comes.

The
Man
Is
Washed.

Then,
Is

Washed
Away,

Dissolved.

And

No
Man

Ever
Was.

Let
The
Thief

In
Your
Story

Transform

Into

A
Crying
Child

You
Fed,

A
Long
Lost
Wanderer

You
Led,

Perhaps
By

A
Single
Word

You
Said.

In
Our
Fear

To
Be
Attacked,

We
Feel,
Anticipate,

A
Return
In
Kind,

Exact,

Of
Our
Own

Unkindly
Act.

The
Silent
Sky

Needs

No
Singing
Bird

To
Call
A
Praise

Unto
A
Name.

Jewels
Stream

Between
My
Fingers,

As,

In
The
Glorious,

My
Heart
Lingers.

No
Happy
Man
Is,

For,
When

Happiness
True
Is
Here,

The
Man

Doth
Disappear.

The
Divine,

Here,
Clear,

Doth
Now
Shine.

All
The
Water,

Wine.

Man

Is
A
Wisp

Of
Gossamer,

Or

Bit
Of
String,

A
Mote

To
Float

Upon
The
Air

Of
Every-
Thing.

The
Drab

Goes.

All
Glows.

Accept

The

Ups
And
Downs

As
Waves

Upon
The
Sea.

They
Neither
Lift,

Nor
Cast
Down

The
Unity,

The
One

Poised

In

Infinity.

Into
The

Infinitesimal

Of
Humility

I
Fall,

And
I
Embrace,

Arms
Beyond

The
Size
Of
Space,

The
Un-
Ending

All.

Perfection
Arrives

In
The
Peace.

That,

Which
Ever
Was,

Is.

And

The
Terrored,

The
Errored,

Has
Lost
Its
Lease.

Let
Awe

Of

All,

One,

Stun.

The
Doors   So
                         Perfect

Blow
Open.   Soft.

The
Doors
Blow
Off,

Are
Tossed
Aloft,

By
Breeze

A
Sanctuary
World

Dawns

Around
A
Man.

Angels
Gather

At
A
Throne.

Things
Sing

One
Name.

Moth
And
Flame,

Gone

Same.

Soul
That
Circled

Round
And
Round

A
Solo
Star,

Now
Spreads
Wings

Unto
Infinity,

And
Is

All
Things
That
Are.

A
Man

Has
Wandered
Off

Unto

The
Mountain
High,

And,
Perhaps,

Into
The
Sky,

Here,

Where
None
Live.

Nor
Die.

Seeker
Asks.

Finding,

Basks.

Man,

Once
Coiled
Afraid,

Now

Lets
Perfection

Pervade.

Old
Troubles,

Swarming
Foam,

Popping
Bubbles,

Return
Home

Into
The
Sea.

(Me.)

Flesh
Grows
Weak.

Mind

Begins
To
Leak,

Soul
To
Seek

The
Door.

The
Silent
Beckons

Infinite
More.

Near
Draws

What
Was

Far
Shore.

Perfection's
Fingers

Hold
The
Day,

Molding
It,

Like

Shaping
Clay.

Matters
Not

What
The
Man

Here

May

Try
To
Say.

I
Surrender
This

All

To
You,

O

Perfect
True.

The
Partialized

Has
Realized,

The
Partial
Eyes

May
Now
Surrender

To

The
Total

True.

Spirit's
Weather
Man

Predicted
This,

A
Blizzard
Storm

Of
Blinding
Bliss,

Perfection's
Kiss

Upon
The
Man

Who

Wandered
Heretofore

Amiss.

Unto

Thy
Holy
Mountain,

Onward
Trod,

O
Man,

Thy
Footsteps
Winding,

Sometimes

Seeming

Somewhat
Odd.

But,
Go,

And
Find

Thy
God.

O
Man,

So
Seeming
Here

So
Terrestrial,

Know,

It
Is
Impossible
For
You

Not
To
Be

The
Infinite

Celestial.

Bring
On
Your
Events,

Wind-
Blown,

O
Great

Unknown.

Bring
On
The

Karma

That
Was
Sown.

All
Of
It,

The
Man
Now

Shall
Own.

O

Seize
The
Moment

That
Sees
The
All.

Unto
Partialities

Refuse
To
Fall.

If
You
Waver,

Unto
The
Perfection,

Call.

Cast
No
Stone,

And
So,

Be
Not

Cast
In
Stone.

Gratitude
Felt,

Fear
Forms

Melt.

The
Soul
Aloft

Follows
After

Ever
Finer
Delight,

Pursuing
Its
Flight,

Ever
More
Soft,

Into
Light.

I

Break
Through
To
You,

My
Love,

Through
The
Thinking,

Through
The
Old

I-Thou
Divide,

Through
The
Old

Yes-No
Collide.

I
Dive
In

To
Your

Perfect
Mellow
Heart,

Where
We

Never
Are,

Never
Were,

Apart.

Hard
Black
Seed

Melts
Open.

Form
Flows.

Blossom
Fragrant
Blows.

Here,
Is
God.

What
Was

Seemingly,

But

Clod,

All

Knows.

Before
Eternity
Occurred,

Before

Anything
Stirred,

Before

The
Word,

When

Not
A
Note

Was
Heard,

We

Are
Here,

Sight

Unblurred.

The
Reality

Of
The

Perfect
Infinite
True

Shines
Through.

Temporariness
Fades

Into

Eternity's
Being.

Blindness
Gives
Way

To
Seeing.

Mystery

Leads
The
Way
Today.

I
Do
Not
Know

Where
Next
I
Go,

Where
Stay,

What
Say.

Sweet
Mystery,

Lead
Forth,

Away.

O
Psalm
Singer,
Sing!

Voice
He
Who

All
Things
Be.

Let
All
This
Day

Pray.

Word
Release

To
Soar
Like
Bird

Into
High
Sky.

Peace.

Let
Man

Be

Today.

Mind

Unwraps
Its
Self,

And
Finds
Inside,

The
Perfect
Present

Present.

Loops
And
Knots

Un-
Done,

Paper,
Ribbons,
Gone,

Little
Card
With
Name,

Tossed,   In
And   The

No   Forevermore.
More,

Mind
Unwrapped

Is
Rapt

I
Stumble

From

Guidance
To
Guidance,

Feeling
Ever

A
Bit
Unaware,

Yet,

Ever,

Feeling
You

There.

O
God,

Guide,

I
Pray.

Show
Me,

Once
Again,

The
Way.

I
Feel
You　　Here.

God,　　So
　　　　Kind,
There.

　　　　In

You　　Your
Lift　　Chair.
Me

And

Place
Me

I
Sit
With
You,

And

What
You
Bring

Brings
Me
To
Sing,

As

You
Are
Singing

Every
Thing.

No
Matter

How
Much
I
Have,
Of
Stuff,

Infinity
Itself

Is
Not
Enough.

Only
Perfect
Love,

O
Perfect
True,

Will
Do.

Only

Loving
You.

Let
Me

Sing
For
Thee.

Let
Breath
Blow.

Let
Heart

Open
Sky
Know.

Let
Stone

As

First
Star
Light
Be.

And

All
Earth,

Sweet
Eternity.

Serenity,

Sweet Friend,

You Arrive

Again.

Man's Noise,

His Silly Play,

Falls Away.

Each Bit Ends.

Heaven's Peace

Comes In,

Transcends.

Let

Rocky
Planet,

Turning

In
The

Day
And
Night,

Ignite,

And

Be

Only
The

Divinity,

In

Man's
Sight.

Damp
And
Cool,

Spring
Can
Appear,

Any
Time

In
The
Year.

And

Any
Where,

Perhaps
Among
The

Harsh
And
Sere.

And,
So,

Here,

A
Fresh

Oasis
Town,

Out
Of
The
Mirages,

Comes
To
Rear.

Let
Me
Hold
Thee,

O
My
World,

Baby
Crying,

Toys
All
Hurled.

In
My
Arms,

Now,

Thou
Art
Curled.

Cease

Thy
Tears.

Rest
At
Peace.

All
Thy
Fears,

Unfurled,

Release.

You
Come
Gently

And

Erase
These
Limits

I
Had
Made
Up.

Silence
Loud

Within
My
Ears,

And

I
Sit
With
You

Forever.

Again.

Man,
Woman,

Go
Their
Way

Upon
The
Earth,

Seeking

What
Is
Worth

Taking
Time

To
Do.

At
Last
Finding

Only

Loving,
You.

A

Sip
Of
Morning
Tea.

A
Wisp
Of

Word
From
Thee.

And

All
Is
Well

In
This

Still
Corner

In

Infinity.

I
Drop

At
Thy
Feet,

O
Peace,
Perfect,

Sweet,

And
Feel

Perfections

Wash,

That
Heal

All
Of
My
Ill,

My
Spirit

Still.

Complete.

O
Listen.

Silence

Has
Become
So
Loud.

Hear
It
Roaring
Now,

Even

In
The
Crowd.

Now
The
Humble,

Filled
With
Grace,

Replace

The
Proud.

The
Planet
Stills.

Quiet
Comes

Upon
The
Town.

The
Infinite
Comes
Down,

And

Looks
Around,

Enjoys.

Time
Has
Gone

Suddenly
Profound,

Sabbath
On
Sacred
Ground.

No
River
Banks

In
Flood

Remain.

No
Shanty
On
The
Shore.

The
Edges

Of
A
Soul,

Where

The
True
Is
Borne,

Now

Are
No
More.

Love
Drowns
All,

Dissolving
Even
The
Stones.

The
Banks
Of
The
River

Quiver

And
Are
Gone,

Only
An
Ocean

Now
Here,

And

Dawn.

ABOUT THE AUTHOR

Who is this Author?

This question is best answered by looking into the author's finished pages, which stand ready for the reading.

But, in the interests of social convention, here is some biographical data to clothe this character.

The early years of the author were steeped in several cultures.

The author as a youngster spent long hours and years in the laconic hard scrabble labor of rural Appalachian mountain life, his father's roots.

The author's mother came from the prosperous flatter farmlands of rural Maryland, close-knit family people of an old Pennsylvania Dutch background, who sang sweet acapela harmonies, while praying and working together.

The author grew up in both influences, while living in the midst of the robust cultural mix of the Washington D.C. environs.

The author left high school blessed with a scholarship to an exceptionally fine university, where he spent his four years, wandering somewhat, among the peaks of Man's intellectual achievement.

The Writing Seminars were among the most memorable experiences of the time there, hours of sharing words among fellow poets, lounging around a large and darkly aged conference table.

In the cultural uproar of the 1968-69 senior year, studies were eclipsed, as the author's interests exploded into off-campus venues and activities, not in the political actions of the day, but in the spiritual, metaphysical and transcendental.

In this vibrant time, the City of Baltimore burgeoned with opportunities for close friendships, learning and practice with various yogis from India, gypsies, highly conscious artists and mystics of various kinds, along with a matured Theosophical Lodge and Rosicrucian Lodge, AMORC, all of this guided by the posters and amazingly well-stocked shelves of the New Age Bookstore, where meditators gathered, crowded together seated on the floor on Tuesday evenings. The author was a part of spiritual communes that started up and renovated spaces in which to work and live together.

This storm of Baltimore life came on, seemed to last forever, and then passed suddenly, with an abrupt departure to a place in Vermont's north woods.

Then stretched decades of living various places, supported by working with hands and small building business activity, with years of life's lessons in family living with children, years of a spiritual-martial practice, years spent close with a guru from India, and years of working with a spiritually oriented mind training course.

In recent years, the art of word-craft, practiced since childhood, came to the fore.

A body of privately written work slowly accumulated, waiting for the writer to feel ready for its release.

FROM THE PUBLISHER

Well, here we are again, with the second book in a series of three. We hope that you enjoy it, as we have again enjoyed putting it together for you.

We still would like to request your help.

If you enjoy *Prayer Sayer Song*, will you please be so kind as to let your kindred spirits know? Will you post a review where you purchased your copy?

Remember, if you have not already done so, you can download your free copy of the Ebook, *Forever Free*.

Get it here:

www.WiseWordWind.com.

You can also sign up there to receive fresh words weekly, in your inbox or on social media, from Ben.

If you would like to connect with Ben, you can email him at Ben@WiseWordWind.com.

Thank you!

-The Team at Wise Word Wind Press

www.ingramcontent.com/pod-product-compliance
Lightning Source LLC
Chambersburg PA
CBHW020517080526
44583CB00013B/628